LEVEL
700L
5 STEP ENGLISH

5 STEP ENGLISH
Puss in Boots

동화
도서출판

5단계로 술술 읽히는 영어원서

단계 영어 장화신은 고양이

초   판 | 1쇄 발행 2025년 10월 20일

지 은 이 | 샤를페로
영어번역 | 신자경, 스티브오
그   림 | M.J 화이트
정보맵핑 | 이야기 연구소
디 자 인 | 임성원
제 작 처 | 다온피앤피
특허등록 | 10-2717987호
국제출원 | PCT/KE202/002551

펴 낸 곳 | ㈜도서출판동행
펴 낸 이 | 오승근
출판등록 | 2020년 3월 20일 제2020-000005호
주   소 | 부산광역시 부산진구 동천로 109, 9층
이 메 일 | withyou@withyoubooks.com
카카오톡 | @도서출판동행

단계별 요약정보 기술은 국내특허등록 및 PCT 국제출원을 했습니다.

ISBN 979-11-91648-52-2 (13740)

Audio Book

5단계로 **술술 읽히는** 영어원서

단계영어

장화신은 고양이

등황
도서출판

언어 실력이 자라날수록,
영어책도 함께 자라야 합니다.

아이에게 신발이나 옷을 사줄 때 한 치수 크게 고르는 이유가 뭘까요? 바로 아이가 빠르게 자라기 때문입니다. 사실 아이의 신체만큼이나 머릿속 사고력도 금방 자라납니다. 그리고 사고력이 자랄수록, 아이가 접하는 영어책도 함께 '성장'해야 합니다.

어린 나뭇가지를 그냥 두면 제멋대로 휘어 자라지만, 어릴 때 곧은 부목으로 지지해주면 올곧게 자라는 것처럼, 아이의 학습도 비슷합니다. 매번 나무를 뽑고 더 큰 나무를 새로 심기보다는, 하나의 나무를 끝까지 가꾸는 법을 알려주는 편이 훨씬 좋습니다. 이 책도 같은 맥락에서 시작되었습니다. **하나의 스토리를 아이 수준에 맞춰 5단계로 발전시키는 신개념 영어 도서이니까요.**

아이들이 말을 배워가는 과정을 떠올려보세요. 처음에는 "엄마", "아빠"처럼 단 몇 단어만 말하지만, 시간이 흐를수록 말이 길어지고 내용도 깊어집니다. 예를 들어, 처음엔 "엄마 밥 줘"라고 말하던 아이가 나중에는 "엄마, 내가 좋아하는 김밥 먹고 싶어요"라고 표현하게 되죠. 중요한 것은 표현이 달라져도 "배가 고파서 음식을 먹고 싶다"는 핵심은 같다는 사실입니다.

이 책의 5단계 영어 구성은 바로 이런 언어 발달 과정을 그대로 담았습니다. 예를 들어, 레벨 1은 네 살 아이의 표현, 레벨2는 다섯 살 아이의 표현과 비슷하다고 볼 수 있습니다. **전하고자 하는 메시지는 같지만, 표현 방식은 점점 더 풍부해지는 것이죠.**

계단을 오르듯이 레벨별로 차근차근 읽어보세요. 아이의 사고력과 함께 영어 실력도 자연스럽게 자라날 것입니다.

스티브 오

As your English skills grow, English books should evolve accordingly.

When you buy shoes or clothes for your child, you often choose a size up because you know they're going to grow. Children's thoughts expand just as quickly, so it makes sense for their English books to evolve as well.

If young twigs aren't supported, they'll grow bent and crooked. However, if you straighten a branch that has fallen to the ground by tying it to a sturdy splint, it will grow upright. Children are no different. Instead of uprooting a sapling to plant a bigger one, teach them to care for the tree they have. This book presents a new approach: it unfolds a story in five stages tailored to different reading levels.

Think about how children learn to speak. A child who can only say "mom" or "dad" soon starts to form longer words and more meaningful sentences. They might first say, "Give me food, Mom," but later, that evolves into something like "Mom, I want to eat my favorite food, gimbap." Even though the words change, the intention—"I'm hungry" or "I want to eat"—remains the same.

In 5 Step English, the natural course of a child's language development—what usually takes three to four years—has been divided into five levels. Level 1 reflects the way a typical four-year-old might speak; Level 2 matches a five-year-old, and so on. The core idea stays consistent, but the complexity of the expression increases with each level.

I encourage you to read through each level as though you're climbing a set of steps, one at a time.

Steve Oh

사용설명서
Manual

영어는 언어입니다. 언어는 암기보단, **실제 사용을 통해 익혀야 합니다.** 즉, 의미가 있어야 하고 내가 사용해야 합니다. 이 책은 학습지가 아닌 책으로서 영어를 의미 있게 사용할 수 있게 제작했습니다.

간단하지만 명확하게 도서 사용방법을 말씀드리겠습니다.

1. 영어 공부가 아닌 **책을 읽는다고 생각하세요.**

2. **레벨 1부터 읽으세요.** 레벨 1이 무척 쉽게 보여도 일단 레벨 1부터 읽어야 다음 단계로 수월하게 올라갈 수 있습니다. 마치 계단을 오를 때, 첫 계단에 발을 내디디고 그 다음 계단으로 오르는 것처럼 말입니다.

3. **모르는 단어가 보이면 사전을 찾지 마세요.** 다시 한번 말씀드리지만, 이건 책입니다. 책은 읽어야 합니다. 우리가 보통 책을 읽을 때 국어사전을 찾으면서 읽지 않는 것처럼 말입니다.

4. **레벨 5까지 읽었다면 이제 레벨 4, 3 순으로 거꾸로 읽어보세요.** 복잡한 문장들이 어떻게 간략하게 요약되는지를 배울 수 있게 됩니다.

사용법은 위 4가지면 충분합니다.

자, 그럼 이제 시작해 볼까요?

※ 레벨5에서는 사전을 찾으셔도 됩니다. 내용 이해를 위해서가 아닌, 모르는 단어의 정확한 의미 파악을 위해 사전을 찾을 필요가 있습니다.

Audio Book Channel

English is a language. Language should be learned through practical use rather than memorization. That means, it has to make sense and you have to use it. This book is not a study book, but a book designed to use English in a meaningful way.

I will tell you how to use the book in a simple but clear way.

1. Do not think that you study English. **Instead, read the book.**

2. **Read the book from level 1.** Even if level 1 looks very easy, you should read level 1 first to move up to the next level with ease. It's just like climbing the stairs. When you go upstairs, you place your foot on the first stair and then go up to the next one.

3. **If you see a word you don't know, don't consult a Dictionary.** Again, this is a book. The book must be read. It's just like we don't consult an English dictionary when we usually read an English book.

4. **If you have read all the way to level 5, now read books backwards in order of level 4 and 3.** You will learn how to concisely summarize complex sentences.

If you have learned above 4 methods, it is sufficient.

So, let's get started, shall we?

목 차
Contents

단계 영어
오디오북 채널

머리말 Prologue

도서 사용법 Manual

Puss in Boots **LEVEL 1**   09

Puss in Boots **LEVEL 2**   39

단계영어

장화신은 고양이

LEVEL 1

단어(Words)

878개

LOW　　　　　　　MIDDLE　　　　　　　HIGH

문장수(Sentences)

143개

LOW　　　　　　　MIDDLE　　　　　　　HIGH

문장길이(Sentence Length)

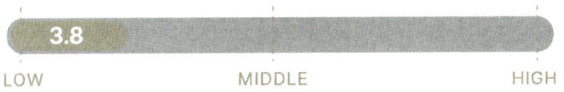

3.8

LOW　　　　　　　MIDDLE　　　　　　　HIGH

읽는 시간(Reading time)

3분 30초

LOW　　　　　　　MIDDLE　　　　　　　HIGH

말하는 시간(Speaking Time)

6분 45초

LOW　　　　　　　MIDDLE　　　　　　　HIGH

Chapter 1

▎The Cat and Three Coins

One day, a father died.

The father had three sons.

The first son got the land.

The second son got the animals.

The third son, Jack, got three
silver coins and a cat.

"I have so little," said Jack.
So Jack decided to leave
home.

The cat spoke to Jack, "Jack, buy me boots and a bag. You will be rich."

Jack bought boots and a bag for Puss.

Chapter 2

Puss went to the forest with Jack.

Jack waited, and Puss caught two rabbits.

Then Puss went to the King's house.

Puss was wearing boots.

People laughed at him.

Puss walked to the King and said, "My dear King, this is for you from my master. These are two rabbits."

장화신은 고양이

The King was very happy.
The King gave Puss a silver coin.
"Say thank you to your master," said the King.

Puss came back to Jack.
Puss showed Jack the silver coin.
"Here, this is for food tonight," said Puss.

Chapter 3
Gifts Every Day

The next day, Puss went to the forest.
This time, Puss caught two birds.

Puss went to the King's house.
"My dear King, this is for you from my master. These are two birds," he said.

The King was very happy.
The King gave Puss a silver coin.
"Say thank you to your

master," said the King.

Every day, Puss caught some animals, and then he gave them to the King.
The King gave Puss a silver coin.
"Thank you. Your master is so nice," said the King.

Chapter 4

Jumping in the Cold River

One day, the King went outside with his daughter. Puss called Jack. "Come on! This is your chance. You will be rich," said Puss.

"Now, go to the river. Take off your clothes and jump into the river. Hurry up," said Puss.

Jack did as he was told.
Puss ran to the King.
"Help me! My master is in the water!" Puss cried.
"What?" said the King.
"Bad people took everything.
They put him in the water. He

will die!" cried Puss.

The King's helpers took Jack
out of the water.
The King gave him beautiful
clothes.
Jack looked great.
The King was happy.
The Princess was happy, too.

Chapter 5

▍"It All Belongs to Jack!"

Later that day, Puss hurried along.
Soon, Puss came to a green land.
He saw some farmers.
Puss made a scary face.
"The King will come here. Tell him this is my master's land," said Puss.

Then Puss went to the farm

Puss saw many cows.
Puss scared the farmer, too.
"Tell the King they are my master's cows," said Puss to the farmer.

Then Puss met a keeper.
He saw many sheep.
"Tell the King they are my master's sheep," said Puss to the keeper.
The farmers and the keeper were so scared.

Chapter 6
❚Tricking the Mean Ogre

Actually, the Giant had all the green land, cows, and sheep.
The Giant was rich and scary.

Puss went to the Giant's house.
When the Giant saw Puss in boots, he laughed.
"What do you want?" the Giant asked.
"People say you are strong and great. I wanted to see you," Puss replied.

The Giant was happy.

"Oh, you saw me. What do you think?" the Giant asked.

"You are the best giant. Do you have magic powers, too?" Puss asked.

"Yes, I have magic powers," he said.

"Can you change into animals?
I want to see it," Puss asked.

The Giant changed into a
lion.
Puss was scared, so he
jumped back.
Then the Giant changed

back into himself.

"Come back, Puss. I will not hurt you," the Giant said.

Soon, Puss came back.

"Mr. Giant, can you change into a small animal like a mouse?" Puss asked.

The Giant changed into a mouse.

Then, Puss caught him and ate him.

Chapter 7

❙The King Thinks Jack is Rich

The King, the Princess, and Jack were happy together in the horse cart.

The horse cart came to the green land.
A few farmers were working.
"This is a good land. Whose land is this?" the King asked.
"Puss' master's land. Puss is

in boots!" said the farmers.
"What? Hey, you didn't tell
me," said the King.
"I forgot to tell you," said
Jack.

Soon, they arrived at the
farm.

상처난훈 고양이

The King loved the cows.

"Whose cows are these?" asked the King.

"Puss' master's cows. Puss is the cat wearing boots," said the farmer.

The King thought Jack was very rich.

Then they came to the keeper.

"They are Puss' master's sheep," said the keeper.

In the forest, a man said, "This is Puss' master's wood."

Chapter 8

❙ A Happy Castle Wedding

They came to the Giant's house.

"Welcome to Jack's house," said Puss.

"This is your house?" said the King.

"Yes, come in," said Jack.

There was a big party in the house.

The King, the Princess, and Jack sat down.

They ate and drank together.

"Jack, you are very rich," said the King.

"Yes, I am very rich," said Jack. "Would you like to marry my daughter?" asked the King.

Jack was so happy.
The Princess was so sweet
and pretty.
Jack already loved her.

"Yes, I will marry her," said
Jack. The Princess liked him,
too.
Jack went to the castle with
the King and the Princess.
Soon, the Princess and Jack
got married.
They lived happily ever after
with Puss.

단계영어

장화신은 고양이

LEVEL 2

단어(Words)

1166개

LOW　　　　　　　MIDDLE　　　　　　　HIGH

문장수(Sentences)

169개

LOW　　　　　　　MIDDLE　　　　　　　HIGH

문장길이(Sentence Length)

6.9

LOW　　　　　　　MIDDLE　　　　　　　HIGH

읽는 시간(Reading time)

4분 39초

LOW　　　　　　　MIDDLE　　　　　　　HIGH

말하는 시간(Speaking Time)

8분 58초

LOW　　　　　　　MIDDLE　　　　　　　HIGH

Chapter 1

❚The Cat and Three Coins

There was a father who had three sons.

One day, the father died. His sons got everything from their father.

The first son received the land and the second son got some

animals. The third son, Jack, was left with only three silver coins and a cat.

"I didn't get much," said Jack. "Oh, leave home and do something," said his brothers.

Jack left home with his cat, Puss.

"Don't worry, Jack. Get me boots and a bag. I will make you rich," said Puss. Jack gave Puss nice boots and a bag.

Chapter 2

Puss Brings Rabbits to the King

"Let's go to the forest. Sit here and wait for me," said Puss.

Puss went into the forest. There were many rabbits there. He caught two rabbits and put them in the bag.

He went to the King's palace. "Can I see the King?" asked Puss. "Oh, you are wearing boots. Interesting! Come in," said the doorman. People laughed at

Puss, but he went in front of
the King.
"My dear King, here's my master's
gift for you." Puss showed the
King two rabbits.

The King was pleased and gave Puss a silver coin. The King asked Puss to thank his master.

Puss went back to Jack. Puss gave him the silver coin.
"Here you are. This might be good enough for tonight," said Puss.

Chapter 3

Gifts Every Day

The next day, Puss went to the forest again. He caught two birds and went to the King with them.

"My dear King, here's my master's gift for you," said Puss. Puss showed the King the two birds.

The King was pleased and gave Puss a silver coin. The King asked Puss to thank his master. Puss then gave the silver coin to Jack.

Every day, Puss caught some animals and gave them to the King. In return, the King gave Puss a silver coin each time.

"Who is your master? And where does he live? He must be so nice," said the King.

Chapter 4

❚ Jumping in the Cold River

One day, the King took a walk with his daughter. Puss went to Jack.

"Let's go, Jack. Hurry up! It's time to take our chance. I will make you rich," said Puss.

Puss and Jack went to the river.
"The King will pass by this river.
Now, take off your clothes and
jump into the water," said Puss.

Jack quickly did it. But the water
was so cold.
"I don't understand," said Jack.

Then Puss ran to the road. The
King was passing by on that road.

"Help! Help! My master is dying in the water," Puss cried.

"What? What happened?" asked the King.

"Oh, my master! Some people hurt my boss. They took every-thing and threw him into the water. He is going to die. He needs your help!" cried Puss.

The King's helpers took Jack out of the water. The King gave

Jack beautiful clothes and made him look like a nobleman. The King was pleased to see him. The Princess was pleased, too.

Chapter 5
"It All Belongs to Jack!"

Puss moved faster than the King's cart. Puss arrived at a green field and saw some farmers. He approached them with a scary face, and the farmers became frightened.

"The King will come soon. Tell him this is my master's land," said Puss.

They said, "Okay, we will do that."

Then Puss met another farmer and frightened him as well.
"Okay, okay. I will say these are your master's cows," said the farmer.

Next, Puss met a keeper with many sheep.
"Okay, I see. I will say these are your master's sheep," said the keeper. Jack finally became the owner of everything.

Chapter 6

Actually, all the land, cows, and sheep belonged to a Giant. The Giant was very rich and scary. But Puss was not afraid of the Giant.

Puss went into the Giant's castle and looked around. When the Giant saw Puss, he laughed. He thought a cat in boots looked funny.

"What do you want?" he asked.

"Everyone says you are a strong and wonderful giant, and I wanted to see you," Puss replied.

The Giant was pleased and said, "Now that you've seen me, what do you think?"

"You are really a wonderful giant. Do you have magic powers, too?" asked Puss.

"Yes, I have magic powers," replied the Giant.

"Can you change into

animals? I want to see that," asked Puss.

"Of course, I can change into animals."

The Giant changed into a big, scary lion. Puss was so scared that he jumped out of the window and ran up to the roof. Then the Giant changed back.

The Giant laughed and said,
"Come back, Puss. I will not hurt
you." Puss returned, still looking
scared.

"Mr. Giant, can you change into
a small animal, too? Is it too
difficult? Can you change into a
mouse?" Puss asked.
The Giant nodded. The Giant
changed into a mouse. He ran,
jumped, and danced around the
room. But he did not last long.
"Ps-s-s-t!" Puss caught the
mouse and ate him up.

Chapter 7

▌The King Thinks Jack is Rich

The King, the Princess, and Jack were talking happily in the horse cart. The King enjoyed talking with Jack. "Go slowly," the King said to the cart driver.

The horse cart arrived at the green land. The farmers were working there.
"This is a good land. Whose land is this?" the King asked.

"It belongs to Puss's master. Puss is the cat wearing boots!" replied the farmers.

"Jack, you are Puss's master, right? This is your land?" the King asked Jack.

"Yes, it's mine. I forgot to tell you," replied Jack.

Soon they came to another farm. The King loved the cows. "Whose cows are these?" asked the King.

"They belong to Puss's master. Puss is the cat wearing boots!" said the farmer.

The King told Jack, "They are great cows." The King thought Jack was very rich. Then they came to the keeper.

"These are Puss's master's sheep," said the keeper.

Chapter 8

A Happy Castle Wedding

They arrived at the Giant's big castle.

"Whose castle is this?" asked the King. Jack could not say anything. Suddenly, Puss said, "Welcome to Jack's castle!"

"So this is your house," said the King.
"Yes, this is my house," replied Jack.

Puss invited them to come inside. They went into the hall. A great dinner was prepared for them.

The King, the Princess, and Jack sat down. They ate and drank together. The King loved the food and the dishes.

The dishes were all made of gold.

"Jack, you are very rich," said the King.

"Yes, I am a rich man," replied Jack.

"What do you think about my daughter? Could you marry her?" asked the King.

Jack was so surprised and happy. The Princess was so beautiful that Jack already loved her.
"Yes, I will marry her," said Jack, and the Princess agreed.

After that, the King and the Princess returned to their castle with Jack. Then the Princess and Jack were married. Puss was also with them, and they lived happily ever after.

단계영어

장화신은 고양이

LEVEL 3

단어(Words)

1708개

LOW   MIDDLE   HIGH

문장수(Sentences)

185개

LOW   MIDDLE   HIGH

문장길이(Sentence Length)

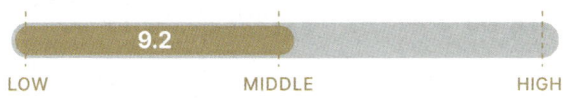

9.2

LOW   MIDDLE   HIGH

읽는 시간(Reading time)

6분 49초

LOW   MIDDLE   HIGH

말하는 시간(Speaking Time)

13분 8초

LOW   MIDDLE   HIGH

Chapter 1

❚ The Cat and Three Coins

There was a grain shop owner who had three sons. When the father passed away, he left his fortune to his three sons. The oldest son received the grain shop and his father's land. The second son received the sheep and cows. The youngest son, Jack, received only three silver coins and a little cat.

"Dear brothers," said Jack, "Puss

is a good little cat, but I don't know how to live on only three silver coins."

"Oh," his brothers replied, "do your best once you leave home."

Jack took the little cat and left home.

"Don't worry, Jack. You have three silver coins. Please buy me a pair of boots and a bag, and I will make you rich," said Puss.

Jack did not want to waste his coins on a cat, but he believed in Puss. Jack went to a shoemaker and asked him to make a pair of boots for Puss. The boots were large enough for Puss and fit perfectly. The shoemaker also gave Jack an old bag.

Chapter 2

▌Puss Brings Rabbits to the King

Puss took Jack into the forest and told him to wait there. Puss ran into the forest, where there were many rabbit holes.

There, he caught two fat rabbits. He put the rabbits in his bag and ran quickly until he arrived at the King's palace.

Puss asked the doorman if he could see the King. The doorman looked surprised because a cat was wearing boots! The doorman was interested in him and allowed him to see the King.

Puss went into the castle, and the people inside laughed at him. Puss didn't care and walked up to the King.

Puss said, "Your Majesty, I bring a gift from my master, the Duke of Carrabas. He sends you these two rabbits. They are for your dinner."

Puss showed him the rabbits and gave them to the King. The King was very pleased and gave him a silver coin. He asked the little cat to thank his master for the wonderful gift.

Puss ran back to Jack and handed him the silver coin.
"There," he said, "let's eat and sleep at an inn tonight."

Chapter 3
Gifts Every Day

The next day, Puss went into the forest again to catch two birds. He brought them to the King.

"These are from my master, the Duke of Carrabas," said Puss. The King thanked the Duke and gave Puss a silver coin. Puss took it to Jack.

장화신은 고양이

"Let's eat and sleep at an inn tonight," said Jack.

Every day, Puss caught some animals in the forest and then took them to the King as a gift. Each time, the King also thanked Puss and gave him a silver coin.

The King thought, "Who is the Duke of Carrabas, and where does he live? He must be a kind man."

Chapter 4

▎Jumping in the Cold River

One day, the King went out for a horse ride with his daughter. Many people in the castle went out with the King.

Puss ran to Jack and cried, "Jack, hurry up! Follow me! Finally, it's time to make you rich!"

Puss took Jack to a river because he already knew the King would be riding by it.

"First, take off your clothes and

hide them under a rock. Then jump into the river," said Puss.

Jack did everything as Puss instructed. The water was so cold that he trembled. Jack had no idea what was happening, but Puss waited and then ran to the road.

Finally, the King was passing by on his horse.
"Help! Help!" Puss cried. "Oh, help! My Lord—the good Duke of Carrabas, is dying in the river!"

"What has happened?" the King asked as he stopped his horse. Everyone, including the Princess, was concerned and listened to Puss.

"Oh, my Lord!" cried the cat. "Suddenly, some thieves appeared and attacked him. They stole everything from him and threw him into the river. If you do not help him, he will die."

The King became alarmed and very worried. He sent the helpers to pull Jack out of the river and gave him a coat. The coat was made of velvet, satin, and gold lace. It was the most beautiful clothing Jack had ever worn. It made Jack look handsome and elegant. The King was so pleased to see how elegant Jack looked.

The King told Jack, "Get into the carriage and sit beside me."
The Princess was pleased with Jack, too.

Chapter 5
▌"It All Belongs to Jack!"

Soon, Puss went ahead of the King's carriage. Shortly, Puss arrived at a field where the farmers were working. Puss walked up to them, pretending to be scary. The farmers became frightened.

"Listen, men," cried Puss. "The King will soon come here with my Lord, the Duke of Carrabas. If the King asks you, say, 'This is the good Duke of Carrabas's land.' If you don't do this,

I will kill you and throw you into the river!" The farmers were so scared. "Okay, we will do as you have told us," they replied.

Then Puss ran until he met a farmer who had cows. Puss scared the farmer, too.

"If the King asks me, I will say these are the good Duke of Carrabas's cows," said the farmer.

A little later, Puss met a shepherd with his sheep. The shepherd said, "I will say these are the Duke of Carrabas's sheep."

Soon it looked like the Duke of Carrabas had everything.

Chapter 6

▌Tricking the Mean Ogre

Everything belonged to a Monster. The Monster was very rich, strong, and scary. A little later, Puss came to the Monster's castle. Puss was not afraid of the Monster and entered the castle. Puss looked for the Monster and soon found him.

When the Monster saw Puss, he laughed a lot. It was so funny to see a cat in pretty boots.

"Who are you, little cat? Why are you here?" the Monster asked.
"I wanted to see you because I heard

you are the strongest and most wonderful Monster in the world."

Hearing that, he became very excited and proud of himself.
"Well, now that you have seen me, what do you think of me?" he asked.
Puss thought that he was a very wonderful Monster. And he had magic powers!
"Can you change yourself into an animal? A lion or an elephant?" asked Puss.

"Oh, yes, that's easy," replied the Monster.

"I want to see that," Puss said. Well, the Monster wanted to show it to Puss.

Quickly, the Monster turned into a lion. He truly had magic powers. The Monster was a fearsome lion. He had thick hair, large teeth, and sharp claws. He roared loudly. Puss was so scared that he jumped out of the window and ran up onto the roof. But he almost fell down because of the boots. There he sat down, shaking so much.

Then the Monster turned back, and he laughed a lot.

"Come back, Puss," he called, "I will not hurt you."

Puss returned to the room, looking very quiet. Puss asked, "Could you turn into a small animal, too? I think it must be difficult. Could you turn into a mouse?"

The Monster quickly turned into a mouse and jumped around the room. "Ps-s-s-t!" Puss quickly caught him and ate him. That was the end of the Monster.

Chapter 7
The King Thinks Jack Is Rich

The King, the Princess, and Jack were riding in the carriage and talking happily together. The King was so glad to talk with Jack. He told the carriage driver to go slowly, so they could have more time together.

The King's carriage passed the field. "That is a wonderful field," said the King. The King asked the farmers who owned the field.

"The good Duke of Carrabas!" answered the farmers.

The King asked Jack, "Duke, you didn't tell me you had a field."
"Oh, Your Majesty, I'm sorry, I forgot to tell you," answered Jack.

Soon after, they came upon a farmer. The King was impressed by the group of cows and asked the farmer who owned the cows.

"The good Duke of Carrabas," answered the farmer. The King praised Jack's cows. The King thought the Duke was rich.

Then they met a shepherd, who said that the Duke of Carrabas owned these sheep. In the forest, a woodsman said that the wood belonged to the Duke. The Duke looked richer than the King.

Chapter 8

A Happy Castle Wedding

Finally, they came to the Monster's great castle. The King asked Jack who lived in the castle. Jack could not answer, because just then, the little cat run out to greet them.

"Welcome, welcome, my lord," Puss cried. "Welcome to the castle of the Duke of Carrabas."

"So this is your house. You live here," said the King. "Yes, this is where I live," answered Jack.

Puss asked them to get out of the carriage.

"I will show you the way to the dining hall," said Puss. The servants had prepared a great feast, as they now served Jack instead of the Monster.

The King and the Princess sat at the table. Jack sat between them. They ate, drank, and feasted until they were full. The King loved the delicious food and the dishes. The dishes were all golden. They were finer than those in the King's castle.

At the end of the feast, the King said, "My dear Duke, you must be very rich."
"I am so rich," answered Jack, "I do

not know how much I have."

"I think," said the King, "you should marry a princess. An ordinary girl is not good for you." Jack wanted to marry a princess, but he desired a perfect one.

"How about my daughter?" asked the King.

When he heard this, Jack was so happy. He jumped with joy. The Princess was so sweet and pretty. He loved her already.

"Yes, she is the perfect princess." And the Princess agreed. So Jack went back with the King and the Princess to his palace, where the two were married and lived happily ever after.

The little cat lived in the palace with them. Puss always stayed by the warm fire and the soft cushion. When Jack's brothers heard about Jack's fortune and how he married a beautiful princess, they thought, "I wish I had kept Puss. I wish I had given Jack the grain shop and the animals."

단계영어

장화신은 고양이

LEVEL 4

단어(Words)

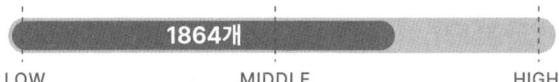

1864개

LOW　　　　　　　MIDDLE　　　　　　　HIGH

문장수(Sentences)

176개

LOW　　　　　　　MIDDLE　　　　　　　HIGH

문장길이(Sentence Length)

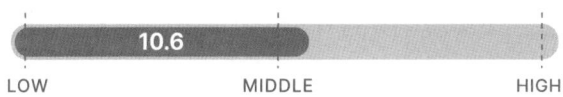

10.6

LOW　　　　　　　MIDDLE　　　　　　　HIGH

읽는 시간(Reading time)

7분 27초

LOW　　　　　　　MIDDLE　　　　　　　HIGH

말하는 시간(Speaking Time)

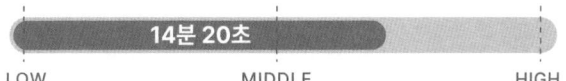

14분 20초

LOW　　　　　　　MIDDLE　　　　　　　HIGH

Chapter 1

❚The Cat and Three Coins

The miller died, leaving his three sons to share his fortune. The oldest son took the mill and the land. The middle son took the sheep and cows. The youngest son, Jack, received only three silver coins and a small cat that lived in the mill.

"I'm happy for you, my brothers," said Jack. "Puss is a nice little cat and can catch mice on his own. However, I don't know how I can live on just three silver coins."

"Oh," said his brothers, "you must now leave home and take care of yourself."

Jack took the little cat and left.

"Don't worry, Jack," said the little cat. "You have three silver coins. Use them to

buy me a small pair of boots and a bag. I will help you make your fortune."

Jack didn't want to spend his money on boots for a cat, but he knew Puss was clever. So, he did what the cat said. He went to a shoemaker, who crafted a handsome pair of boots for three silver coins. They fit Puss perfectly. The shoemaker also gave Jack an old bag that he no longer needed.

Chapter 2
▌Puss Brings Rabbits to the King

Puss led Jack to the countryside and told him to sit by the road and wait. Then, the little cat ran into the forest, where many rabbits lived. Puss caught two big, fat rabbits, put them in the bag, and walked to the King's palace in his neat little boots.

A cat wearing boots was such an unusual sight that the King agreed to see him

immediately. The King's helpers and guests whispered and laughed when they saw the cat enter the room. But Puss walked straight to the King and bowed deeply.

"Your Majesty, my master, the Duke of Carrabas, has sent you a gift of these two good, fat rabbits for your dinner," said Puss, taking the rabbits out of the bag and giving them to the King.

The King was delighted. He gave Puss a silver coin and asked the clever cat to thank his master for the wonderful gift.

Puss ran back to Jack and gave him the silver coin. "Here," he said. "This is enough for lodging at inn and dinner tonight."

Chapter 3

❚ Gifts Every Day

The next day, Puss went to the forest again. This time, he caught two fat birds and took them to the King.

"These are gifts from my master, the Duke of Carrabas," said Puss.

Once again, the King thanked the Duke and gave Puss a silver coin. The clever cat brought it back to Jack, and it was enough for food and a place to stay.

Day after day, Puss caught some fine game in the forest and brought it to the King as a gift from the Duke of Carrabas. Each time, the King thanked Puss and gave him a silver coin. The King grew curious about the Duke of Carrabas. He wondered who this generous man was and where he lived.

Chapter 4

▌Jumping in the Cold River

One day, the King went for a ride with his daughter and many helpers. Puss rushed to Jack in excitement.

"Come quickly!" he cried. "We've done a great job so far, but now is the time to make your fortune!"

Puss took Jack to a river where he knew the King would soon pass by.

"Take off your clothes and hide them under that rock," Puss said. "Then stand in the water up to your neck."

Jack did as he was told, even though the water was icy cold and made him tremble. He had no idea how this would help him earn any money.

Puss waited until Jack was standing in the river. Then, he quickly ran to the road where the King's coach was approaching.

"Help! Help!" exclaimed Puss. "Please help! My master—the noble Duke of Carrabas—is drowning!"

The King stopped his coach at once. The Princess, the guests, and the helpers all leaned forward to listen.

"What happened?" asked the King.

"Oh, Your Majesty!" Puss cried. "My honorable master was attacked by thieves.

They stole everything and threw him into the river. Without your help, he will surely drown!"

The King was very worried. He quickly ordered his helpers to pull Jack from the river and dress him in fine clothes of velvet, satin, and gold lace. It was the first time Jack had ever worn such fine clothes.

When the helpers brought him to the King, he looked handsome and noble. The King was so pleased with Jack's appearance that he invited him to sit beside him in the coach. The Princess was delighted with Jack.

Chapter 5

▮ "It All Belongs to Jack!"

Meanwhile, Puss raced ahead of the King's coach. Soon, Puss reached a field where farmers were harvesting grain. He walked up to them with an angry look,

making his whiskers puff out so he looked twice as big. The farmers were scared.

"Listen, everyone!" shouted Puss. "Soon, the King is going to pass by with my master, the Duke of Carrabas. If he asks who owns this field, say it belongs to the noble Duke of Carrabas. If you don't, I'll beat you and throw you into the river!"

The farmers were so scared that they agreed to do what Puss said.

Puss kept running until he saw a farmer with a large field of cows. Puss scared him

into promising to tell the King that the field belonged to the noble Duke of Carrabas.

Later on, Puss met a shepherd with his sheep. The shepherd also promised to say that his sheep belonged to the Duke of Carrabas. Puss kept doing this until it seemed like everything belonged to the Duke of Carrabas.

Chapter 6
▌Tricking the Mean Ogre

All these things belonged to a rich, strong, and terrifying Ogre, but Puss wasn't afraid of the Ogre at all.

After a while, Puss reached the Ogre's castle and went inside. He ran through several rooms until he found the Ogre sitting there.

When the Ogre saw the little cat wearing shiny, creaking boots, he burst out laughing. He had never seen anything like it before.

"Where are you from, my good little cat?" the Ogre asked.

"Oh, it's far away. I'm from over the

hills," Puss replied.

"And what brings you here?"

"I just wanted to meet you because I heard you're the strongest and most amazing Ogre in the world."

The Ogre was thrilled because he was very proud of himself. "Well, you saw me, what do you think?" the Ogre asked.

Puss said he thought the Ogre was truly amazing. Then he asked, "Is it true that you have magic powers?"

The Ogre proudly confirmed that he did.

"Can you turn yourself into an animal if you want? Like a lion or an elephant?" Puss asked.

The Ogre said, "Oh, yes, that's easy!"

"I'd love to see you do it," said the cat.

The Ogre was happy to show him. He immediately turned into a lion, as he really had that power. He became a fierce lion with a thick mane, big teeth, and sharp claws, roaring loudly.

Puss was so scared that he jumped out the window and climbed up the roof, even though his boots made him slip. He sat there, spitting and shaking with fear.

The Ogre changed back to his real shape and laughed loudly. "Come back, Puss," he said. "I won't hurt you. Now you see that what you heard is true."

Puss slowly came back into the room, looking scared and shy.

"Yes, I see that it was true," Puss said. "But, Mr. Ogre, can you turn into a small animal too? That must be a lot more difficult. Can you become a mouse?"

The Ogre could do that too. Right away, he turned into a mouse and started running and dancing around the room. But he didn't dance for long.

"Ps-s-s-t!" With one quick leap, Puss caught the mouse and ate him before he could make a sound. The Ogre was gone.

Chapter 7

❚The King Thinks Jack Is Rich

Meanwhile, the King, the Princess, and Jack rode together in the fancy coach, talking happily. The King enjoyed talking with Jack so much that he told the driver to slow down, so they could have a good time together.

The King's coach passed by a field where farmers were working.

"What a fine field of grain," said the King.

He leaned out of the coach and asked the farmers, "Who owns this field?"

"The noble Duke of Carrabas!" the farmers answered.

The King looked at Jack. "Duke, why didn't you tell me this field was yours?"

"Oh, I'm sorry. I forgot to tell you," Jack replied.

Soon, they passed by the owner of the cows. The King was impressed by the large

herd of cows and asked the owner, "Who owns these cows?"

"The noble Duke of Carrabas," the owner replied.

The King looked at Jack and praised him for his animals. He thought the Duke must be very rich.

Next, they met a shepherd, and the King asked the same question—the sheep belonged to the Duke of Carrabas.

In the forest, the woodcutters said the trees belonged to the Duke. It looked like the Duke was richer than the King.

Chapter 8
▌A Happy Castle Wedding

At last, they arrived at the Ogre's big castle. The King wondered whose castle it was. The grand doors stood open, and Puss appeared at the entrance.

"Welcome, Your Majesty," Puss said. "Welcome to the Duke of Carrabas's castle."

"Oh, this is your home!" said the King.

"Yes, this is my home," Jack replied.

Puss asked them to step out of the coach and led them to the big dining hall. There, the servants were preparing a wonderful meal because now Jack owned everything in the castle.

The King and the Princess sat at the table, with Jack between them. They ate, drank, and enjoyed the meal until they were full. The King had never tasted such delicious food served on golden plates before. Those plates were even finer than the King's own.

After the meal, the King turned to Jack and said, "Duke, you are a very wealthy man."

"Yes, I am so rich that I don't even know how much I have," Jack replied.

"Indeed," said the King, "How about marrying a princess who would be a worthy partner?"

Jack liked the idea of marrying a princess, but he wanted to be sure she was
the right match.

"Then what about my daughter?" asked
the King.

When Jack heard this, he felt like jumping
with joy. The Princess was so kind and
beautiful that he already loved her. "Yes,
she would be the best in the world," he said.

And the Princess said yes.

So Jack returned to his castle with the
King and the Princess. There, Jack and the
Princess got married and lived happily ever
after.

The little cat stayed in the castle with them. Puss always had the softest cushion and the warmest spot by the fire. When news of Jack's good fortune reached his brothers, they regretted not keeping Puss. They wished they had given Jack the mill and the animals instead.

단계영어

장화신은 고양이

LEVEL 5

단어(Words)

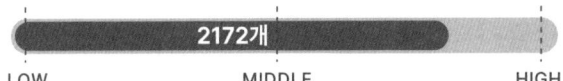

2172개

LOW   MIDDLE   HIGH

문장수(Sentences)

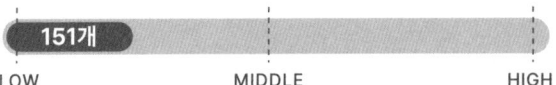

151개

LOW   MIDDLE   HIGH

문장길이(Sentence Length)

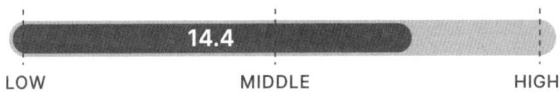

14.4

LOW   MIDDLE   HIGH

읽는 시간(Reading time)

8분 41초

LOW   MIDDLE   HIGH

말하는 시간(Speaking Time)

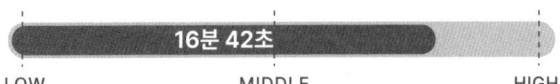

16분 42초

LOW   MIDDLE   HIGH

Chapter 1
❚The Cat and Three Coins

A miller died, leaving his three sons to divide his fortune among themselves. The eldest son took the mill and the land around it, and the middle son took the flocks of sheep and herds of cows. All that was left for the third son, Jack, was only three pieces of silver and a little cat that lived in the mill.

"I'm happy for you, my brothers," said Jack. "Puss is a fine little cat and can feed on the mice he catches, but I do not see how I am to live on three pieces of silver."

"Oh," answered his brothers, "you will have to leave home and make your own way in the world."

Jack took the little cat and started out. "Don't worry, Jack," said the little cat. "You have three silver pieces. Take them and buy me a little pair of boots and a bag, and I will make your fortune for you."

Jack did not want to spend his money on a pair of boots for a cat, but he knew Puss was a wise little animal, so he did as he said. He went to a shoemaker, and for the three pieces of silver the shoemaker made the prettiest pair of little boots ever seen; when Puss put them on, they fit perfectly. The shoemaker also gave Jack an old bag that he no longer wanted.

Chapter 2

▌Puss Brings Rabbits to the King

Puss led Jack out into the country and then asked him to sit down by the roadside and wait for his return. The little cat ran off into the nearby forest, where there were many rabbit holes, and there he managed to catch two plump rabbits. He put the rabbits in the bag and made his way in his neat little boots until he came to the King's palace.

There he asked to see the King, and a cat wearing boots was such a strange sight that he was brought to see his Majesty right away. The King's advisors and guests nudged each other and laughed when the cat entered the court, but Puss marched up to the King and bowed deeply before him.

"Your Majesty, my master, the Duke of Carrabas, has sent you a present of these two plump rabbits for your supper," said Puss, as he took out the rabbits and presented them to the King. The King was delighted. He rewarded Puss with a piece of silver and asked the little animal to thank his master for the splendid gift he had sent.

Puss ran back to where Jack was waiting and gave him the piece of silver.
"There," he said. "That is enough to pay for a bed and a supper at the inn.

Chapter 3
❚Gifts Every Day

The next day Puss set off for the forest again, and this time it was a pair of plump partridges that he caught and carried to the King.

"They are sent by my master, the Duke of Carrabas," said Puss. Again the King sent his thanks to the Duke and gave Puss a piece of silver, which the little cat carried back to his master, and it was enough to buy Jack food and lodging.

This routine continued with impressive consistency. Every day Puss caught some fine game in the forest and took it to the King as a gift from the Duke of Carrabas, and every day the King thanked the cat and gave him a piece of silver.

The King began to wonder who the Duke of Carrabas was and where he lived. He began to think the Duke was a very generous fellow.

Chapter 4

▌Jumping in the Cold River

One day the King went out for a pleasure ride with his daughter, and many of his courtiers rode with him. Puss rushed to his master. "Come quickly!" he cried. "We have done well enough so far, but the time has now come when I will make your fortune."

The cat then led Jack to a river where he knew the King would pass before long. He told Jack to take off his clothes, hide them under a rock, and stand in the river up to his neck. Jack did this, even though the water was so cold it made him shiver. He did not know how Puss was going to make his fortune in this way.

Puss waited until he saw his master standing in the river, and then he ran to the road where the King was riding.

"Help! Help!" he cried. "Oh, help! My master—the

noble Duke of Carrabas! He will surely drown."

"What is the matter?" asked the King as he stopped his coach, and the princess, along with all the courtiers and guards, listened.

"Oh, Your Majesty!" cried the cat. "My noble master! He was attacked by robbers. They robbed him of everything and threw him in the river, and without help, he will surely drown."

The King was deeply concerned. He sent guards to pull Jack from the river and dress him in robes of velvet, satin, and gold lace. Jack had never worn such fancy clothing before, and he looked handsome and noble when he was brought to see the King. The King was so pleased with how Jack looked that he ordered Jack to get into the coach and sit beside him. The Princess was even more pleased with Jack than her father.

Chapter 5

▋"It All Belongs to Jack!"

Meanwhile, the little cat had hurried far ahead of the King's coach. Presently, Puss came to a field where the farmers were harvesting the grain. Puss marched up to them, scowling fiercely and puffing up his whiskers until he looked twice as big. The farmers were frightened.

"Listen, men," cried Puss. "The King will soon come this way with my master, the Duke of Carrabas, riding beside him. If he should ask you whose grain this is, answer that it belongs to the noble Duke of Carrabas. If you do not do this, I will tear you to pieces and throw you into the river!"

The farmers were so frightened that they promised to do exactly as Puss told them. Then Puss ran on until he met a rancher driving a great herd of cattle. Puss frightened him too, and the rancher promised that if the King asked whose herd these were, he would say it belonged to the noble Duke of Carrabas.

A little farther on, the cat met a shepherd with his sheep, and he also promised to say that his flocks belonged to the noble Duke of Carrabas. So it continued. Soon it seemed as though everything belonged to the Duke of Carrabas.

Chapter 6
▌Tricking the Mean Ogre

In truth, all these things truly belonged to an Ogre who was very rich, fierce, strong, and terrible, and after a while, Puss arrived at the castle where the Ogre lived. The little cat was not afraid of Ogres. He made his way into the castle and ran from room to room until he found the Ogre sitting.

When the Ogre saw the little cat in his fine, shiny, creaking boots, he was so amused that he laughed aloud. He had never seen such a sight before. "And where did you come from, my fine little cat?" he asked.

"Oh, from over the hills and far away."

"And what do you want here?"

"I only wanted to see you because everyone says you are the strongest and most wonderful

Ogre in all the world."

Upon hearing this, the Ogre was overjoyed, for he was very vain. "Well, now that you have seen me, what do you think of me?" he asked.

Puss thought the Ogre was truly wonderful. And was it true that he had magic powers, too? And did he truly possess magic powers? Yes, the Ogre did.

"Can you transform yourself into an animal of your choosing—say, a lion or an elephant?" asked Puss.

"Oh, yes, that is easy enough," replied the Ogre.

"I would like to see you do that," said the cat.

Well, the Ogre was willing to show him. At once he turned himself into a

lion, for he really had that power, and he was a ferocious-looking lion indeed. He had a thick mane, giant teeth, and sharp claws, and he roared loudly. Puss was so terrified that he jumped through the window and scrambled up the roof, though he almost slipped and fell because of his boots. There he sat, spitting and shaking with fear.

Then the Ogre turned himself back into his original shape, and he laughed heartily. "Come back, Puss," he called, "I will not hurt you. Now you see that everything they told you was true."

Puss came scrambling back into the room, and he looked very meek and timid. "Yes, I see it is all true," he said. "But, Mr. Ogre, could you turn yourself into a small animal as well? That must be much harder. Could you turn yourself into a mouse?"

Yes, the Ogre could do that, too, and immediately he turned himself into a mouse, and ran—skipping and dancing around the room. But he did not skip for long.

"Ps-s-s-t!" With a bound Puss caught him and swallowed him whole before he could even squeak, and that was the end of the Ogre.

Chapter 7
▌The King Thinks Jack Is Rich

Meanwhile, the King, the Princess, and Jack rode together in the fine coach, talking pleasantly. The King was so pleased with his conversation with Jack that he told the coach driver to go slowly, so that they could have more time together.

The King's coach rolled past the field of grain where the farmers were at work. "That is a fine field of grain," said the King, and he leaned out of the coach, calling out to the farmers and asking who owned the field.

"The noble Duke of Carrabas!" answered the

farmers.

The King turned to Jack. "My dear Duke, why did you not tell me it belonged to you?"

"I had forgotten," answered Jack.

Soon after, they came to the rancher. The King admired the herd of cattle and asked the rancher who owned them.

"The noble Duke of Carrabas," answered the rancher.

The King turned to Jack and complimented him upon his herds. He began to think that the Duke must be very wealthy. Then they came to the shepherd, who said that his flocks belonged to the Duke of Carrabas. In the forest, the woodsmen said the wood belonged to the Duke. It seemed as though the Duke was richer than the King himself.

Chapter 8
▌A Happy Castle Wedding

At last, they arrived at the Ogre's grand castle, and the King asked Jack who lived there. Before Jack could answer, the doors were thrown open, and the little cat ran out onto the road.

"Welcome, welcome, Your Majesty," Puss cried. "Welcome to the castle of the Duke of Carrabas."

"So this is where you live," said the King.

"Yes, this is where I live," answered Jack.

The cat invited them to get out of the coach and led the way into the castle's grand dining hall. There, the servants had prepared a magnificent feast, for now Jack owned everything in the castle.

The King and the Princess took their places at the table, and Jack sat between them. They ate, drank, and feasted until they were full. The King had never tasted more delicious food, and it was all served on golden plates that were much nicer than those in the King's own castle.

At the end of the feast the King turned to Jack and said, "My dear Duke, you must be a very rich man."

"I am so rich," answered Jack, "that I really do not know how much I have."

"It seems to me," said the King, "that you should marry a princess, for an ordinary girl would not suit you."

Yes, Jack would like to marry a princess, but it would have to be the right princess.

"Then what about my daughter?" asked the King.

When he heard this, Jack was ready to jump with joy, for the Princess was so sweet and pretty that he loved her already. "Yes, she would do better than anyone else in the world," he said, and the Princess said yes.

So Jack went back with the King and the Princess to the King's palace, and then the Princess and Jack were married and lived happily ever after.

The little cat lived in the palace with them. The softest cushion and the warmest corner by the fire were always left for Puss. As for Jack's

brothers, when they heard about Jack's good fortune and how he had married a beautiful princess, they wished they had kept Puss for themselves and given Jack the mill and the livestock instead.

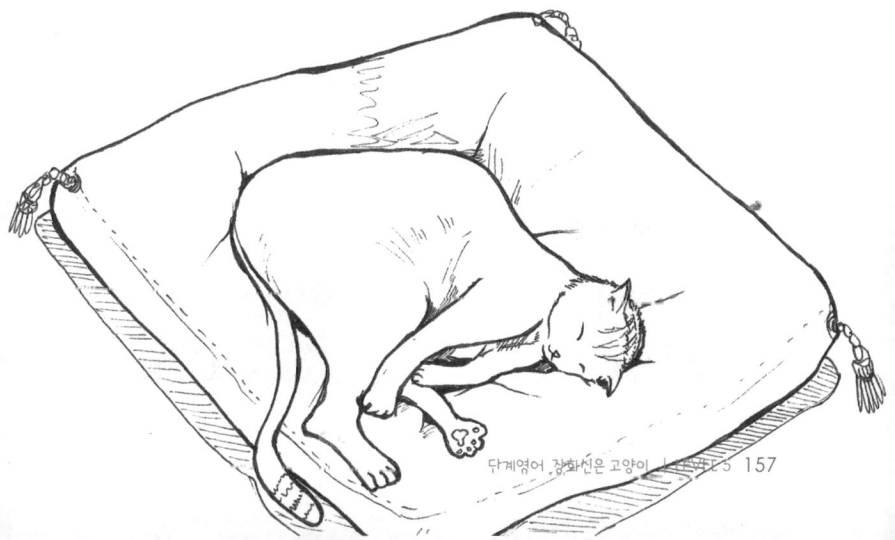